The Agile Manager's Guide To

HIRING EXCELLENCE

By Hardy Caldwell

Velocity Business Publishing
Bristol, Vermont USA

Copyright © 1998 by Velocity Business Publishing, Inc.

All Rights Reserved

Printed in the United States of America

Library of Congress Catalog Card Number 97-81353

ISBN 1-58099-006-1

Design by Andrea Gray

Title page illustration by Elayne Sears

If you'd like additional copies of this book or a catalog of books in the Agile Manager Series™, please get in touch with us.

- **Write us at:**
  Velocity Business Publishing, Inc.
  15 Main Street
  Bristol, VT 05443 USA

- **Call us at:**
  1-888-805-8600 in North America (toll-free)
  1-802-453-6669 from all other countries

- **Fax us at:**
  1-802-453-2164

- **E-mail us at:**
  info@agilemanager.com

- **Visit our Web site at:**
  http://www.agilemanager.com

The Web site contains much of interest to business people—tips and techniques, business news, links to valuable sites, and electronic versions of titles in the Agile Manager Series.

Call or write for a free, time saving "extra-fast" edition of this book—or visit www.agilemanager.com.

Contents

Other Books in the Agile Manager Series™:

Giving Great Presentations
Understanding Financial Statements
Motivating People
Making Effective Decisions
Leadership
Goal-Setting and Achievement
Delegating Work
Cutting Costs
Effective Performance Appraisals
Writing to Get Action
Building and Leading Teams
Getting Organized
Customer-Focused Selling
Great Customer Service

Introduction

There are few things more important to the organization you work for, or to your career, than to hire strong, capable people. Good people are the bones and muscle of any organization, including your department or group. Hire well, and your job becomes easier.

Yet there are few things more difficult to do than hire well. It takes skill, experience, and a system.

This book will give you some of the skills, a taste of the experience, and a system.

Why a system? It keeps you from doing something otherwise-smart managers do all the time: Hire by the seat of their pants. They may have a vague idea of the kind of person who will fit a particular job, and they may feel they are good judges of character. So they "wing" interviews and end up hiring on superficial characteristics like looks, personality, credentials, or golf handicap.

The seat-of-the-pants method leads to mistakes—sometimes big, expensive mistakes. I myself used it for years. Sometimes I was lucky, which emboldened me to keep using it. Then a string of bad hires, for which I paid dearly (and daily), caused me to go about hiring in a more systematic manner. I hired better.

A system also involves you in all stages of the hiring process. That's essential if you want consistently good results. When you rely on outsiders like the human resources people or a personnel agency to screen and sometimes hire candidates, you often end up taking what you can get. (And you get what you deserve.)

Hiring throws a lot of managers because it's not an objective task. People are not objective. You think you're hiring skills and experience, and maybe you are. But you're also hiring attitude, beliefs, values, and personality.

And these aspects are just as important as skills and experience. Proof? People rarely get fired because they can't do the work. They get fired because they are abrasive, risk averse, know-it-alls, and a host of other personality-based reasons.

This book will help you discover the skills and experience each candidate might bring to the job. It'll also help you gain insights into the all-important people aspects.

The Agile Manager's Guide to Hiring Excellence presents time-tested and innovative information in a form designed to go down easily, so you don't waste time. You can read it in a few sittings, then keep it nearby for reference. You'll find useful tips and techniques you can put to use on the job today.

Plan Your Hiring Strategy

"[Most] people are more incompetent than you probably expected—certainly more so than their résumés or they themselves led you to believe."

V., IN *THE MAFIA MANAGER*

Chapter One

*T*ake the Time to Hire Right

The Agile Manager pondered the problem yet again. He sighed.

No getting around it, he thought to himself. I need to hire another person. We have too much documentation now to keep sending the work out of house.

The Agile Manager headed product development for a division of a large company. He prided himself (as did the company) on keeping his department lean. Fewer people, he knew, meant a bit more money for all in his group, fewer management hassles, and a more tightly knit team. He hired only as a last resort.

But the spreadsheet on his computer screen told the story. He figured he'd save $15,000 a year by hiring a combination writer/graphic arts person to produce user manuals and other documents relating to the products the department created.

And that's right off the bat, he thought. Considering the three new products due out this spring, using outsourcers to produce the documentation will cost even more.

OK, I'll do it. But this time I'm going to dig for more references, that's for sure.

The Agile Manager still smarted over his last hire, a product designer who shone brightly in the interview, whose references couldn't say enough good things about her, and who, it turned out, had the work ethic of a sloth. She usually came in late, and occasionally not at all. And when you talked to her about it, she adopted a prima donna attitude that said, "You're lucky to have me. Don't question the way I work." Never mind that her manner of working produced little of value.

The Agile Manager reduced the pain of the memory by recalling the startled look on her face when he fired her, but that was another story . . .

While the quote that leads off this section is overstated, it's not too far off the mark. That's why it's important to take the time to hire right. Hiring poorly can cause you hours of grief.

And it's expensive. Look at what hiring costs:

Time. You spend time:

- Thinking about what you want and what the job requires
- Finding prospects
- Interviewing
- Checking references
- Negotiating a deal.

Training. Few people can hit the ground running. Some companies have training programs for new employees that stretch over the course of a year. These are costly to set up and administer.

Money. Each new hire gets a salary, as well as benefits worth perhaps 15 to 25 percent of the salary.

Lost time. Lost time comes in two flavors. It is, first, the time a new recruit spends on the job unproductively. This might be a few days, or a year.

Second, if the new person fails, you've lost all the time and training you put in, plus you have to start all over again.

Add together all these items, and the bill can range from $10,000 for a lowly hire to $100,000 or more for a senior executive.

And don't forget the cost to your body and soul. A poor employee can cause more sleepless nights and foul moods than just about any other business problem.

Hire the Best

Decide, now, you're going to hire the best. You'll put in a lot more work on hiring than perhaps you have been, but it'll more than pay off in lower employee turnover, greater productivity, better results, and sleep uninterrupted by job concerns.

Decide, too, to use your human-resources department sparingly. Use it—maybe—to find candidates for you (while maintaining your own sources), to test for basic job skills, and to ensure the legality of all you're doing.

You know best what you need to succeed. Don't pass off such an important job to someone who doesn't and can't know your exact needs as well.

Track measures that tell how well you're hiring. Doing so improves your skill.

Hiring the best, incidentally, isn't usually a matter of offering the most money. Most excellent people will work for less money in exchange for greater responsibility or a greater opportunity.

Track Your Costs

One way to get better at hiring—and to produce evidence that you're getting better—is to track some measures that indicate the efficiency and overall success of the hiring process.

First, keep a log of the amount of time you spend on each hiring job, together with related costs like advertising or using a personnel service. At the end of the process, multiply the time you spent by your total hourly compensation. Then add in hard costs. The figure may scare you. If so, whittle it down by concentrating on the most important tasks in the process and becoming more skillful at them.

Second, keep track of employee turnover from year to year. Figure that by dividing employee terminations in a year (for whatever reason) by the average number of jobs. If you lose five people out of fifteen, for example, your turnover is .33.

Third, track tenure on the job. If the people you hire tend to stay no more than two or three years, figure out what it would take to increase that number. You'll gain in many ways. (The U.S. median length of job tenure for all men, incidentally, is 4.0 years. It's 3.5 years for women.)

Tracking these measures serves as a reminder that hiring is expensive—and also that you can get better at it.

Trust a System, Not Your Gut

Don't use your intuition or psychic abilities to make a hiring decision. Intuition has a place in hiring, as you'll see. But few of us are quite the judges of skill and character that we think we are. And none of us can know the future.

That makes hiring tough. Even if you pick a great person with a terrific track record, something may be going on in his or her private life that impairs job performance.

Best Tip

Use a system to hire well. Those who "wing" the hiring process often fail miserably.

Go through the process this book describes. It won't guarantee you the perfect person for the spot you have available—nothing can—but it'll go a long way toward reducing mistakes. And it may well keep you from making a career-damaging blunder.

The Agile Manager's Checklist

✔ Decide to hire the best. In the long run, it'll ease your work life and make you more promotable.

✔ Measure the success of your hiring methods. Nothing beats hard facts to improve your skills.

✔ Avoid using your intuition alone to hire. Rather than trust your gut, trust a system.

Chapter Two

Assess Your Workplace

"Hey Steve!" The Agile Manager yelled to his assistant on the other side of the wall.

"Yeah, boss?" said Steve entering the office expectantly.

"I'm about to write a job description for the documents position. But I'm thinking to myself, wait a second. Every job has a context—the department, people, the whole company. Defining the context will help me figure out what kind of person we need, and it'll give that person an idea of our culture. Does that make sense?"

"I guess. But most people won't care about the context—they just want a job."

"Right—but they should care about the context. I remember my second job, with Applied Matrix. It was a real button-down place with about six levels of managers for only 150 employees. I should never have taken that job. They booted me after nine months."

"You got fired?" asked Steve incredulously. He'd never heard anyone admit that out loud before.

"Well, yeah. It was mutual, but they asked me to leave before I told them where to go. Anyway, I wish the guy who hired me had said something like, 'I want to tell you about this place. Every morning we salute the CEO, then the flag. Everybody wears a white shirt and a red tie. If you wear brown shoes, you're out. If you try to

outflank the chain of command, you're out.' If he had done that, I wouldn't have taken the job. It would have saved us both trouble."
"I get it," said Steve. Make sure you have a good fit. But if you only get people like us, won't that turn us into a bunch of sheep?"
"Hmm," said the Agile Manager stroking his chin. "Good point. Well, we're all different. I guess it's about making sure that we agree on the large things—like being honest in work, working hard, advancing on merit rather than seniority, and so forth."

When hiring, you first need someone who can do the job. Just as important, you need someone who will fit in with your group. This has nothing to do with color or religion or where the person grew up or went to school. It's all about company culture and the values that shape it.

Getting a good fit, also, has nothing to do with conformity or ensuring everyone thinks about things the same way. Some organizations do demand conformity in appearance and thinking. In the long term, they tend to have troubles.

Your job is to ensure that there's nothing about your organization—mission, values, unwritten rules—that a newcomer would find impossible to adapt to (unless you're looking to shake up the place). Doing the following quick exercises, mostly in your head, will give you a benchmark that will enable you to put the job in context and, come interview time, assess a candidate's answers concerning values and job expectations.

Assess the Culture

You may know, down to the last detail, the important things about the organization you work in: its mission, values, and cultural characteristics. Maybe some of these things, like the mission, have been published in the newsletter or employee manual.

If they haven't been written down, or you haven't thought about the subject, you can still identify them. The signs are all around you. Doing so is important if you're going to find a person who doesn't have to fight the culture just to get a job done.

Values, for instance, exist whether written down or not. To uncover values, ask:

- *What rules do people live by?*
- *Who gets ahead and why?*
- *What do senior executives and the CEO talk about all day?*

Answers to these questions will help you identify values. Here are some examples.

Positive values: We ship orders same day. We always meet our financial goals. We practice total, complete honesty in all dealings. Every employee is to be in on decisions that affect them. We share the wealth. Customers above all. People advance on merit.

Neutral values (could be useful or not): We are totally disciplined. We are messy and creative. We have fun at work. Work is serious business. We respect the hierarchy. We circumvent the hierarchy in service of the customer.

Unconstructive values: Cover your butt. Always take credit when you can. Undermine anyone in marketing. Tell customers lies if it gets them off your back. Never contradict the boss.

A lot of what you'll come up with will be neutral values. These characterize what your workplace culture is like—it's neither right nor wrong, it just *is*.

When you know your values, you can better assess whether a candidate has a chance of a long-term tenure with the company.

Assess Reputation and Working Conditions

Companies compete for good people. Sometimes it's hard to remember this, especially when fifty people apply for each position. It's important, therefore, to assess your company's reputation and working conditions.

Maybe you're known as a creative place that doesn't pay well yet offers interesting work. Or you pay well but tend to be slow-moving and bureaucratic.

And it's worth remembering that while you may love your converted (yet trendy) garage located downtown, others may prefer the gleaming six-story buildings just off exits 22-27 of the Beltway that your competitors inhabit.

Know your company and what you're up against. Such knowledge may help you attract a certain kind of candidate, or cement a deal with someone who's wavering. ("Sure you'd make more money at ACME. But you'll have thirteen bosses breathing down your neck, and you'll need a form signed in triplicate to get a pencil. Here you'll be your own boss—and I'll buy you a box of pencils your first day.")

Assess Yourself and Your Group

Finally, think carefully about all the people in your group, especially their personalities and characteristics and how you all interact. What makes you work well together? Shared interests? Ambition? Desire to remain safe and secure? Are you a serious bunch? Pranksters?

Know the values you and your group live by. It'll make it easier to choose a new hire.

Maybe you all interact poorly or your results are spotty. Think about what kind of person would help break logjams and improve morale. Here's where you might wish to bring in someone with new, fresh values. Wonderful things happen when you hire a new person with the right chemistry to change or enliven the rest of the group.

The Agile Manager's Checklist

✔ Plan to hire someone who can do the job—but also someone who will fit in with your group.

✔ Assess your workplace by analyzing mission, values, and cultural characteristics.

✔ Know how your company's reputation stacks up with that of competitors.

Chapter Three

Assess the Job

The Agile Manager sat in the meeting room with Wanda, his second-in-command, and project supervisors Phil, Anita, and William.

"So Phil," said the Agile Manager, "right now you hire independent contractors to do five manuals a year. Anita, three manuals. William, six manuals and about ten monthly product-update sheets."

He continued. "I don't think there's any doubt we could use someone. And now we're keeping products going an average of eighteen months longer than we did, say, five years ago. That means we need to revise about thirty manuals every year. Right?" He looked around the table.

"So where we gonna put her?" asked Phil.

"Her?" said Wanda, arching her eyebrows. "Why is it a 'her'?"

"I don't know. I always think of a graphic designer as a woman. No offense meant."

"Offense taken," said Wanda. "The world will be so much happier when we stop pigeonholing people according to their sex."

"Sorry," said Phil, looking bewildered behind his thick lenses.

"Now," said the Agile Manager. "What are we going to look for in this person? Anyone ever hire a writer/designer before?"

17

"I did once at my old job," said Anita. "I can tell you it was hard to find someone who could write and design. I hired a good writer, then made her"—she avoided looking at Phil—"learn to use a desktop-publishing program. It took a while, but eventually she got it right."

"The writing part is more important," said Wanda, looking around the table. "If we have trouble finding a combo person, we'd better do what Anita did: Hire the writer and then send them for training in graphics."

After assessing the overall workplace, it's time to consider the purpose and details of the job you're hiring for.

Nail Down the Job's Particulars

The questions in this section will help you begin to figure out the skills and personal qualities you need in a jobholder.

Doing a comprehensive job answering the questions makes the rest of the process easier. You'll know exactly what skills and other characteristics you're looking for in the candidates you interview.

What's the purpose of the job? What are the results you expect? If you can't boil the answer to these questions down into one sentence, rethink your desire to make a job available. I've worked in places that have hired people because the common sentiment was "We need another person." That's not fair to the person you hire, nor to your organization.

You should be able to put the job into concrete terms, like these:

- "This person will work on new-product development and be expected to oversee the introduction of at least five new products each year."
- "This person will take Carol's place in customer service, entering an average of fifty orders a day and handling ten customer phone calls."
- "This person will do research on the aerospace industry and make recommendations to investors that are right more than they are wrong."

What's the daily work of the job? This is the job description, which you'll use to identify skills needed and create classified ads. Be as specific as possible about daily tasks and routines, reporting structure, occasional duties, and how the work will be accomplished. For example:

> The new hire will become an expert on the companies in the aerospace industry by reading financial reports, staying in touch with senior company officials by phone and in person, and by developing and maintaining industry and academic contacts. He or she will use this information to make buy/hold/sell recommendations on companies in the industry for the benefit of clients.
>
> The jobholder will issue approximately fifteen recommendations per month. In addition, he or she will be expected to "sell" recommendations to institutional investors and speak to the media regularly about industry-related investment issues.
>
> The jobholder is on call all hours of the day or night to major clients. Past jobholders have worked fifty-five to sixty-five hours a week. The jobholder reports directly to the manufacturing analysis group's vice president and should expect to travel five to seven days per month and do occasional weekend work.

To come up with such a detailed description, talk to the person now holding the job. Keep in mind, however, that the current or just-past jobholder shaped the job around his or her skills and idiosyncrasies. You see may see opportunities to change the job so it provides greater benefits for the company.

What if the job is a new position? Start with the results you're seeking, then identify the tasks

Best Tip

First, define exactly what the purpose of the job is. Then identify exactly what the results should be.

that will produce them. Take the time, however, to think through how the job will integrate with and affect others.

Do you need to fill the job? At this point, anyone interested in efficiency and productivity should stop and ask: Do I need someone in this position? Can I parcel out the tasks to other people in the group? Can I restructure a couple of jobs to avoid hiring?

People complicate matters. The fewer needed to accomplish goals, the better.

Rank the job's characteristics in order of importance. Now rank the characteristics you outlined in the job description in order of importance. These are the tasks or results that the jobholder will be judged on. Keep the list to four to six items.

Using the example above:

1. Make useful recommendations that result in gains for clients.
2. Sell to institutional investors (generating commissions of at least $250,000 yearly).
3. Be on call to give advice to investors.
4. Speak with the media and express the company's point of view succinctly and professionally.

Making this list strips out the "how" of the job (travel, hours worked, research done, etc.) and focuses your attention on the "what" of the position—the aspects of the job that provide value.

Chart the Job's Achievement Factors

Use your list of the job's most important characteristics to come up with another list—the jobholder's probable "achievement factors." These are the skills, abilities, and personal characteristics a candidate should have to ensure success in meeting the goals of the job. Take each characteristic one by one:

Make useful recommendations that result in gains for clients. Analytical and research (investigative) skills, education in financial management or accounting (with an MBA), human-relations skills, insight into the psychology of markets, ability to work alone productively, good writing skills, knowledge of the aerospace industry, interest in business and investing, integrity, decisiveness, willingness to work all the hours necessary to make good recommendations.

Sell to institutional investors. Sales and presentation skills, enthusiasm, human relations skills, poise and tact, proper corporate appearance, inner drive to succeed at sales.

Be on call to give advice to investors. Willingness to serve at any hour, client orientation, human-relations skills, ability to think on one's feet, decisiveness, understanding of investors' needs.

What skills and other qualifications must your new hire have? Rank them in importance.

Speak with media and express the company's point of view succinctly and professionally. Role awareness (looking and acting like an expert), excellent communication and human-relations skills, enthusiasm for subject, ability to simplify and summarize complex issues, having the wisdom and ability to avoid verbal traps and subterfuge, ability to take a stand.

As you can see, the achievement factors are a mixture of hard skills or tangible items like degrees earned, experience, and personality characteristics and values.

If you're having trouble coming up with a list, think about people who have held the job before. Why were (or weren't) they good at it?

You might want to keep this list on your desk for a few days. You'll add to it as new concerns pop into your mind.

Pick the Achievement Factors

Most—maybe all—of your candidates won't have all the achievement factors. Your eventual pick, however, should have the important ones. Rank eight to ten in order of importance.

It's around these factors that you'll plan your interview.

Be careful with this list. You don't want it to keep you from selecting a person who might do well. Be absolutely certain you need these qualities.

In our example:

1. Aerospace industry experience.
2. History of profit-making securities recommendations.
3. Demonstrable skills in research and analysis (information gathering, sifting/analyzing, and arriving at a decision/point of view, for example).
4. Excellent writing and speaking skills, including presentation skills.
5. MBA in accounting or finance.
6. Looks/acts the part of industry expert.
7. Demonstrable sales skills/experience.
8. Decisiveness (willingness to take a stand).
9. Able to travel, work long hours.

If you can come up with only six or seven factors, fine. Beware, however, of going beyond ten. If you overdefine the job, you'll make your search much harder.

Be Firm—and Flexible

Plan to hold to your most important factors when picking a candidate.

Yet be flexible in coming up with them. For instance, I've always found it useful to be flexible with things like education and experience. Why, for example, is a college degree absolutely necessary if someone acts like they have a degree and more than enough experience to make up for it?

You've defined a job to be done. Find a person who can do it. Beware of adapting the job to a particular person.

But don't ever forget that a job is a set of tasks that need to be performed to get results. Executive recruiter John Wareham (speaking of high-level hires) believes you should be prepared to fit the job to a good person. Peter Drucker, on the other hand, believes you must keep trying until you find the right person for the job as you define it.

Drucker further points out that jobs interact. If you change one to fit a candidate, it changes the jobs of others and disrupts work. I'm with Drucker on this one. Hiring right should impose discipline. If a candidate can't do certain tasks, who will? Fitting the job to the candidate can open a can of worms.

Be Aware of Legal Issues

While we'll be discussing legal issues in detail in the next chapter, here's something to keep in mind: Your achievement factors and job qualifications must not in any way discriminate based on race, color, nation of origin, marital status, religion, sex, age, sexual orientation or preference, or disability. In choosing a person for a job, you must choose based on skills, credentials, experience, and ability alone.

Figure a Salary Range

You've defined a job with objective duties and results. You've identified what the person in it needs to do to succeed. Now set a salary.

Sometimes figuring a salary or wages is easy—you run a union shop or your organization mandates a certain salary for anyone in the position for which you're hiring.

If not, you'll have to do some thinking. First, don't automatically pay the new person what the old jobholder made. Maybe it was too little, or maybe it was too much. I once hired someone for an important job, a newly created position, who lasted less than a year. The next jobholder came in at nearly twice the salary of the last person. We needed to boost salary that high to get someone with the right skills to succeed.

Don't pay a person the least you can get away with. Pay enough to keep a good person in the job for a long time.

If you don't know what to pay someone, look in the classifieds. See what other, similar jobs pay. Talk to your human resources people. Talk to people in noncompetitive companies. Call your state's department of labor. Talk to those in your industry or professional group.

Beware your urge, however, to pay more than is necessary. You might think that paying at a certain level will motivate the person to expend more effort to do well.

Pay motivates to a certain extent. But bringing someone in at a higher level than you need to serves little purpose. The salary soon becomes an entitlement to the jobholder. It also sets a higher ground level for subsequent pay increases.

I like to pay close to competitive rates, while offering greater opportunity to advance and bonuses based on merit. You may not have such flexibility.

Put Achievement Factors on Paper

Create a worksheet like the one on page 59 in chapter eight. You'll need to refer to the achievement factors occasionally between now and the interviewing stage. Then, in the interview, you'll base your questions on them and rate candidates by how well they fulfill your requirements.

The Agile Manager's Checklist

✔ Define the purpose of a job and write a detailed job description.

✔ Ask yourself, at least once, "Do we really need to fill this position?"

✔ Identify and rank in importance the job's characteristics.

✔ Chart the job's achievement factors—the skills, experience, and personal characteristics you'll look for in candidates.

✔ Figure a salary range that's high enough to attract better-than-average candidates.

Chapter Four

Stay Within the Law

The Agile Manager, leaning back in his chair and letting sunlight flood his face, closed his eyes and let his mind wander. It meandered back to that time about fifteen years ago when he chose not to hire Billy Harris for a sales job.

"He's fifty—too old," said the Agile Manager to his boss. "This job demands a young person. Look at what it involves—traveling to at least a dozen trade shows a year. Besides, I want somebody with all his wits. What are we supposed to do when he slows down or has a heart attack? I want somebody I can count on for the long-term."

His boss, Merrill Schmidt, seemed to think anything the Agile Manager thought or did was fine. "OK. But who are you going to hire?"

"Well, I just interviewed this hotshot just out of C-Corp's management training program. He already knows he doesn't like the culture there, and we'd get him all trained and ready to go . . ."

The Agile Manager's eyes popped open. He liked to face reality, but it was tough remembering this event. That "hotshot," it turned out, had actually been fired by C-Corp for his lousy attitude, the same thing the Agile Manager fired him for six months later.

And poor Billy Harris, the Agile Manager thought. No, poor me. He's still going strong at age sixty-five. He has a lot more energy than some of the campus slugs I interview each fall. I really did him wrong—and put the company at risk at the same time. We're lucky we didn't get slapped with an age-discrimination suit. I wonder how I ever made it this far . . .

Hiring in the United States is subject to dozens, if not hundreds, of laws. These range from laws imposed at the federal level to those instituted by states, and cities or towns.

Most of these laws are well-meaning attempts to remove any hint of bias from the hiring process. They do a good job of that—maybe too good a job. Even when you've done nothing wrong, you still can't help but wonder. Sometimes you may feel you must hire a less-qualified person of a certain race or with a disability just to avoid the appearance of bias. (Don't worry—you don't.)

Think of employment laws as objects in an obstacle course. If you know the objects and the course, you can run it swiftly and fluidly, even in the dark. If you don't know either, you could be in for the surprise of your life.

Best Tip

Keep a good employment lawyer on call. He or she can warn you away from a multitude of hiring traps.

We'll cover some of the basic legal aspects of hiring in the next few pages (and the legality of reference checking in chapter ten). Be aware that the laws mentioned cover all aspects of hiring—setting wages, recruiting, interviewing, reference checking. Never lose sight of them throughout the process.

There's no way, however, any book can cover all the laws pertaining to your geographical location or industry. That's why you need, as part of your team, a good employment lawyer. He or she will know all the applicable laws depending on your situation and can answer questions, review documents, and provide counsel on all aspects of hiring and employment.

Federal Laws

Most of these laws have to do with a lot more than just discrimination in hiring. They cover promotions, pay, firing, work environments, training, etc. But here we'll stick to hiring.

Title VII of the Civil Rights Act. This is the big one. It prohibits discrimination in hiring based on race, color, religion, sex (including sexual harassment), or national origin. While it applies to organizations with fifteen or more employees, you may well have state laws covering organizations with fewer people. (And besides, people can still sue you over civil rights based on other documents, like the U.S. Constitution.)

This Act gives you an out if you can prove it necessary. It says: "It shall not be an unlawful employment practice for an employer to hire and employ employees . . . on the basis of [their] religion, sex, or national origin in those certain instances where religion, sex, or national origin is a bona fide occupational qualification reasonably necessary to the normal operation of that particular business or enterprise . . ."

The Americans with Disabilities Act. Part of this lengthy act says you can't discriminate against a "qualified person with a disability because of the disability." It is, further, unlawful to ask whether a person has a disability or to talk about an obvious one. It's also against the law to require a medical exam before making a job offer. (You can require a medical examination after hiring—and even condition the offer on successfully passing the exam—as long as everyone in that job category has to take one.) The ADA covers organizations with fifteen or more employees.

Never forget: Employment laws cover all aspects of workplace practices and conditions—not just hiring.

The Equal Pay Act. You must offer equal pay for equal work. You can't pay different wages or salaries based on sex.

The Age Discrimination in Employment Act. This act, which covers organizations with twenty or more employees, says you can't discriminate against employees aged forty and over.

Focus on the Job

The intent of these laws is the same: To encourage employers to focus on the job and its tasks, not on the person doing it. (Or the person you're contemplating hiring to do it.)

It's not that hard to avoid trouble. All you have to do is ask yourself, "Does this interview question or recruitment action have to do with qualifications or on-the-job performance?" If not, drop it like a hot potato.

Focusing on the achievement factors you came up with in the last chapter will help keep you clean. They are objective hiring criteria. Just make sure you apply the factors equally to all candidates.

Best Tip
Keep all hiring-related practices and questions focused on the job and the results you need.

The achievement factors are your backup, too, if someone alleges discrimination. If a person says, "You didn't interview me because I'm fifty-five," you can say, "On the contrary, we didn't interview you because you didn't have ten years' retail sales experience."

Get the Information You Need

How can you get around these laws? You can't. But you can still get answers to important, job-related questions. In the case of considering hiring someone with a disability, for instance, don't assume the disabled person can't do the job. That's discrimination. Instead, describe the job and ask whether (and how) the applicant can perform it—never making reference to the disability. If the disabled person can perform the job, you have no grounds to deny him or her that chance (based on the disability alone).

If you're interviewing an obviously pregnant woman, you can say, "This job requires traveling one week out of the month. Is that a problem for you?" The applicant may disqualify herself immediately, or she may say, "Not at all," knowing she has a nanny all lined up.

Summing Up: Forbidden Questions

Unless you have a really good (and legal) reason, don't get anywhere near:

- Religion
- Marital status
- Sex
- Disabilities
- Race
- Color
- National origin
- Sexual orientation or preference
- Children
- Age
- Questions about labor union activities

Internet Employment Resources

The Internet is filled with sites linking you to employment law and analysis. Check out the following:

Employment and benefits law: *zeta.is.tcu.edu/~yancey/emp_law.htm*
Laws enforced by the EEOC: *www.eeoc.gov/laws.html*
The Internet Legal Resource Center: *lawlinks.com/ar-areas.html*
Society for Human Resource Management: *www.shrm.org/hrlinks/legal.htm*
The U.S. House of Representatives Law Library: *law.house.gov/100.htm*

To Test or Not to Test

Pre-employment testing is another legal can of worms. You can usually test as you please, but keep a few things in mind:

- *The test must be job-related.* What's job-related? You must be able to show that the results of an achievement test, for example, predict on-the-job performance.
- *Everyone applying for a job must be subject to the same test and graded on exactly the same scale.*
- *The test must not discriminate.* What's discriminatory? Good question. Many people feel that intelligence or aptitude tests inherently discriminate against anyone who hasn't had the benefit of a good education (like many inner-city residents). This is, to say the least, a murky area.
- *The test should reflect the job.* In other words, don't give people a difficult aptitude test for a job lifting boxes.

Whatever kind of testing you're considering, *get your attorney's opinion.* There are probably industry regulations and state or local laws that affect what you can do and how you can do it.

Useful Kinds of Tests

That said, let's look at some of the tests at your disposal.

Ability or skills tests. These are the kind I like. It's hard to fake it if you don't know the answer.

Use ability tests whenever you can to ensure the prospective hire has the skills you need. For example, give prospective secretaries a typing or filing test. Have a candidate for a copier maintenance position break down a machine and put it back together. Give a candidate for bookkeeping work an exam to test facility with numbers. Have a prospective trainer do a training session.

Such tests aren't always applicable or available for higher-level positions, but use your ingenuity. It can be worth your time.

I once was in on the hiring of a candidate for an editorial position at a publishing house. We were about to offer our top choice a job when I suggested testing the skills we thought he had.

Were we ever stunned to find out this person—with a graduate degree in English—could neither write nor spell! And we were a hair's breadth away from offering a job.

Drug tests. This is probably the messiest of all testing areas. Courts at all levels and jurisdictions decide cases and create new precedents on a near-daily basis.

Drug testing is sometimes mandated by the government. The U.S. Department of Transportation, for example, requires drug and alcohol testing of truck drivers and those in "safety sensitive" positions like bus drivers and airline pilots. The regulations also allow random testing, something illegal in other industries.

Testing in such situations seems reasonable. Yet many people say that any drug testing is an invasion of privacy and that, besides, it's difficult to get accurate results. A person may test positive for drugs based on prescription or over-the-counter medicines, for example, or for no good reason at all.

Nonetheless, it's estimated that 20 percent of employees in the U.S. are subject to drug testing of one kind or another. Done right, a drug-testing program can keep you from hiring people who could become problem employees. Consult a lawyer if you're going to set one up. If you design a program poorly, you could subject yourself to a defamation, wrongful discharge, invasion of privacy, or negligence suit.

Test for skills or abilities. (But make sure you give everyone the same test.)

Lie-detector tests. The Employee Polygraph Protection Act of 1988 prohibits you from giving lie-detector tests. And you can't discriminate against anyone who refuses to take one.

This Act does, however, exempt a number of businesses, like the security, pharmaceutical, or precious commodities (gems) industries, among others.

Honesty tests. If you can't give polygraph tests, what can you do? Give a written honesty test. Some companies specialize in them. Be prepared to pay well for a good one (and perhaps for a consultant to interpret results for you).

Many people question the value of such tests, feeling that a smart but dishonest person could pass with flying colors.

Less-Than-Useful Tests

I have trouble with intelligence, personality, and other psychology-oriented tests for the following reasons:

- The results are open to interpretation.
- Many of them offer no proof that they are valid.
- What about people who are poor test takers? Or good ones? Both groups distort results.
- If you like to hire people who do well at a certain kind of test, are you creating a company or department of clones? Good managers know that lots of different personality "types" can succeed in certain occupations.
- Some managers let tests make hiring decisions for them. They can, they know, always point to the test results if things go poorly with the hire.

Part of a manager's skill lies in divining—in person—the kinds of things these tests purport to uncover for you, like personality traits, underlying ambitions, or general intelligence.

With the interviewing methods this book describes, you should be able to get firsthand knowledge of all these things. And you'll develop something else—your own wisdom and skill in understanding people, identifying their strengths, and uncovering driving forces.

The Agile Manager's Checklist

✔ Always review hiring laws before you begin a search.
✔ Keep in mind, especially, Title VII of the Civil Rights Act, the Americans with Disabilities Act, the Equal Pay Act, and the Age Discrimination in Employment Act.
✔ Test for skills and abilities (typing speed, programming skill, etc.) when you can. Be wary of psychological tests.

Find and Screen Candidates

"Don't surround yourself with people who are like you: strive for difference and diversity."

RICHARD MORAN IN *NEVER CONFUSE A MEMO WITH REALITY*

Chapter Five

*F*ind Great Candidates

"Terry," said the Agile Manager, feet up on desk, twirling the phone cord. "I'm looking for a person to do documentation for us. Thought you might know of somebody."

"Hmm," said Terry, head of human resources for a nearby software company. "I've seen a lot of them come and go here recently. Nobody I'd recommend. It's like they all learned how to do a newsletter on Microsoft Word, then began calling themselves 'desktop publishers' or 'document-creation specialists.' Actually, the real problem isn't in knowing the software or coming up with an acceptable design—it's the writing. I've had only one person in the past five years or so that was a really good writer."

"That's key for us. We need someone who can understand what our products do and write simply and professionally. But the person also has to be able to use design software—our marketing people are too busy to handle our jobs."

"Have you advertised yet?" asked Terry.

"No. I'd rather avoid that. I always think of advertising as dragging the ocean with a net—you get way too much junk. Also, an advertisement always brings in at least a hundred résumés. I get confused."

"Here's an idea," said Terry. "Try Ted Garafolo at Monument Graphics. He's president of the Valley Design Professionals. It's a networking group of just the kind of people you're interested in. If nothing else, he can announce the opening at the next meeting."

"Hey, thanks a lot. I'll do that." I knew I could get something good from her, thought the Agile Manager.

Finding good candidates for your job is time-consuming work. But it's well worth it.

Too many managers take the five or six candidates sent over by human resources or an employment agency and pick the "least worst" for the position. Or they choose from a pool of résumés brought in by an ad.

Either of these methods might help you find a gem once in a while. But you'll mostly get duds. Go out and shake the trees yourself—and deputize your people to do the same.

Use Your Own Methods

Using personnel agencies or your own human resources department to find candidates is purely reactive. You wait for a good person to pass by you, rather than going out to find one on your own. And that's usually what you have to do to hire well.

Don't rely on your HR department to find good candidates for you. Go out and find some of your own.

Use these methods to find good people:

Networking. Always be on the lookout for good people, even when you don't have a job open. If you bump into a good prospect at a mixer or industry meeting, exchange business cards. Write on the back what interested you about the person. If you do this often enough, soon you'll have a bulging file of potential candidates when a job opens up.

When you definitely have a position to fill, call your friends, both in the company and out. They might not have names on the tips of their tongues, but they'll know people who might.

Keep an eye out in-house. First, look in your own department. Are any of your people capable? Then look into other departments. Do you see any bright prospects in there or in other company locations?

If you see potential hires toiling for another manager, use all your tact pursuing them. "Stealing" other managers' bright stars won't earn you their lasting friendship.

Here's where a good HR manager can help out. Mention that you have your eye on so-and-so and that you could use some help setting up an interview without ruffling feathers.

Post a job announcement in-house. See who shows interest. But be aware that hiring in-house has its downside.

I once interviewed three current employees and hired one of them for a production job. Doing so created two problems:

—The two that didn't get hired got mad and took it out on the one that did.

—The one I hired didn't work out. I had to "fire" her, sending her back to her old job. She never forgot the humiliation.

Turn your people into recruiters. Some companies offer employees cash bonuses for finding people to fill jobs. Some (like Cypress Semiconductor and Merck) make it a management task.

Your own people are good recruiters because they'll be attracted to people they would find easy to work with. And if you're managing well, they'll search with your high standards in mind.

High-school counselors and teachers. If you have to fill minimum-wage jobs, go to the local high school. Counselors and teachers know who the good kids are. Maybe you'll find a few who stay with the job longer than three months.

Radio advertising. A local software company advertises on the radio—and for some pretty high-level jobs. The ads run quickly through positions available, but their emphasis is on an 800 number that gives more information on jobs available.

The Internet. The Internet is revolutionizing job posting and job searching. Could you possibly cast a wider net than in cyberspace? These are among the most prominent matchmakers:

The Monster Board: *www.monster.com*
Yahoo: *www.yahoo.com/Business_and_Economy/Employment/Jobs*
E-Span: *www.espan.com*
On-line Career Center: *www.occ.com*.

In addition, if you have a company web site, create a section devoted to job openings. (For ideas on how to structure it, visit the Web sites of just about any large company.)

Senior centers. In Florida and other havens for retirees, the "boy" bagging groceries might be sixty-seven years old. Older workers are often wiser and more stable than the crop of sixteen year olds you now depend on for low-wage jobs.

To find older workers, post notices at houses of worship, senior centers, and state employment bureaus.

Recruiters, Personnel Agencies, HR Departments

Should you use a recruiter or agency or your in-house personnel department to find candidates? Sure—but don't relax your own efforts. Continue gathering names on your own.

Best Tip

Advertise jobs on your company's Web site. You'll get computer-literate candidates.

Executive recruiters. Organizations use recruiters—headhunters—mostly for high-level positions or those that have a large impact on the company's success. Recruiters can be valuable because they work to entice good candidates who aren't necessarily looking for a job. As one recruiter said, "By definition, we carry them kicking and screaming from their old positions into the new one."

Recruiters get paid a percentage, usually 25 to 35, of the recruit's yearly salary. For really important jobs—like finding a CEO—they may get more, plus expenses. Also, the best of them often work on retainer. They get paid whether they land a person or not.

A good recruiter will assess your needs and workplace thoroughly and work hard to find a good match. You can count on a recruiter to produce a handful of highly qualified candidates.

Yet there are quite a few fly-by-night operations among the ranks of executive recruiters. Before using one, check references and speak to satisfied customers.

Personnel agencies. Companies often use personnel agencies for lower-level administrative and unskilled positions, especially when they don't have their own human resources people.

Personnel agencies generally get paid only when they place a person with your organization. The fee is usually a percentage of the job's yearly salary—anywhere from 10 to 25 percent.

Best Tip

Avoid personnel agencies, except those that specialize in a particular industry.

Unlike recruiters, most agencies send you candidates that have come to them looking for a better job. They have, therefore, a changing inventory of candidates. Upon rare occasion they'll dig out candidates that haven't come to them.

The biggest problem with agencies is that they send unqualified people. You have a good defense to fend off unwanted bodies: the job description and list of achievement factors you created in chapter three. Use them to avoid wasting time interviewing people who couldn't possibly fill your position.

Human resource departments. If you're fortunate, you have really good human resources people who will sit down with you and discuss in detail the position you're trying to fill. They will come up with an excellent strategy to pull in the right candidates, going way beyond sticking an ad in the paper. They will prescreen and test candidates for you, keeping all the legal considerations in mind. In short, a great HR manager can be like having an in-house recruiter.

If you have an average or overworked HR manager, however,

you'll get the basics: five to eight candidates, all culled from the files or attracted by an ad.You might get lucky, but probably not.

To get the most out of your in-house personnel people, produce your job description and a list of key achievement factors. Let them know you have high standards and you want really good candidates. Get mad at them if they send unsuitable people for interviews. If you can, approve the ads they write up. Better yet, write them yourself.

State employment bureaus. These are kind of like government-run personnel agencies. They only thing to recommend them is the price—their services are usually free.Yet they might be just the thing if you suddenly have to hire a hundred laborers for six-month positions.

Tips on Advertising

Don't forget the old workhorses of searching for candidates— space ads and classified ads. These work—both for you and the candidate. (I've hired good people through ads, and I myself once got an excellent job by responding to one.)

Let's run through a few tips for writing ads.

Write the ad with your job description and list of achievement factors in front of you. Don't try to put everything in— just the top two or three items in each category. And be specific—your goal isn't to get a huge number of respondents. It's to get a handful of candidates well-suited to the position.

Be thoroughly professional. Good people are put off by poor ads—those that are incomplete, unattractive, or vague.

Sell the job and company. Some companies put their mission in an ad, and some lead with a line like, "Be part of the future at XYZ Corp.!" Good people don't just want a job, they want to sign on to a cause, something larger than themselves. Your sales job is especially critical if it's for a low-level or minimum-wage job. Dress it up as best you can: "Flexible hours!" "Be your own boss!" "The hippest restaurant on the planet!"

Put your ad in a trade magazine first. You'll increase your chances of getting a pool of people with the right skills and experience.

Put the ad in Sunday's paper. It's the best read by those seeking jobs.

For low-level or minimum-wage jobs, make it easy to apply and interview. "Call Jim anytime, or drop in between 10 and 2."

Forget blind ads, those without a company name attached. Good people want to know who they are writing to. Besides, they'll wonder, what if I tip my hand to the wrong person?

Consider putting in the salary range. It'll cut down on the number of people responding to the ad. (Unless it's high. Then it will attract more people.)

Use phrases like "good opportunity," and "great working conditions." You want to engage people, so a little mystery goes a long way.

Ask for samples of work when you can. Some jobs lend themselves well to prescreening through samples, like design, writing, advertising, etc.

Need good examples of effective ads? Buy the Sunday paper and see which ones catch your eye.

The Agile Manager's Checklist

✔ Cast a wide net when gathering names of job candidates. Among the best methods: network, search in-house, and turn your people into recruiters.

✔ For higher level jobs, consider using a headhunter. Good ones can be worth their weight in platinum.

✔ Make your classified ad graphically pleasing and textually enticing. Scan the paper for models.

Chapter Six

$\mathcal{S}$creen Candidates

The Agile Manager sighed and stared at the inch-high stack of résumés before him. All from the Valley Design Professionals. He said aloud, "Are none of them happy in their jobs?"

A quick riffle through the pile displayed a pattern that answered his question. Seventy-five percent of them were from free-lancers who were no doubt tired of hustling for jobs and ready to settle down to a regular paycheck.

About half, he noticed, sent samples of one sort or another. Good, he thought, that makes the job easier. I should ask everyone we're interested in to send samples. We should be able to spot a lack of talent in no time.

He whipped through the pile in about five minutes, putting aside those without the right skills. Most of these were artists and designers who either didn't understand the all-important writing component of the job, or who pretended that writing was the easy part. He took that pile and swept it into the garbage can next to the desk.

Then he began studying each cover letter/résumé combination.

Can't write a sentence, he thought. Out.

Writes poetry only. Out.

Two typos in an otherwise good letter. Out.

Good letter, good experience. In.
Wants to save the world. Out.
Shows an awareness of accuracy and speed. In, definitely. . . .

If you've done a good job recruiting, you have a pool of qualified candidates to choose from. Begin to evaluate them.

Screen with Achievement Factors

Use the job's achievement factors as a filter through which to
look at résumés and cover letters. If you don't, you'll begin to
relax your standards.

Relaxing standards is usually a subtle process. "Hey, look at
this person," you'll think. "He doesn't have sales experience, but
he was in marketing for ABC Inc. I bet he's got some experience
we could use."

You may also get blinded by impressive credentials. ("She went
to Harvard! She must be pretty smart.") Credentials are like pedi-
grees in the canine world. Pedigree or no, the dog may be mean,
lazy, or useless. (And people, like mature dogs, don't change. Never
believe, for instance, that you can turn a nonproducer with good
credentials into a star.)

Before You Evaluate . . .

Don't make too much of the
résumés, cover letters, and appli-
cations you evaluate. As author
and hiring expert Robert Half
says, "A résumé is a balance sheet
without any liabilities." Half also

|Best Tip

When screening candidates,
don't relax your standards.
You set them for good, job-
related reasons.

maintains that he doesn't see a correlation between a résumé
and job performance. Good candidates, he says, sometimes refuse
to spend time on it, while poor candidates invest all their time
and wiles to make themselves look like something they are not.

Résumés and cover letters can, at best, only hint at the capa-
bilities of the person applying for the job. Your real work in

finding a suitable candidate comes in the interview, when you can dig deep to identify skills and attitudes, and to expose weaknesses.

That's why you shouldn't be too rigid in evaluating résumés and cover letters. Drop from consideration people who clearly aren't suited to the position, but give those you're unsure about the benefit of the doubt.

Look at résumés in batches, spending no more than an hour at a time with each batch. Otherwise you may fall asleep with your eyes open.

Evaluate the Cover Letter

Cover letters are revealing. To harvest their fruits, ask yourself:

Does the applicant understand the position being offered? Despite the information you provided in your ad or networking call, many people will write letters that sound as if they were applying for a completely different job. One reason: Careless job hunters create "form" cover letters—one size fits all. Look for genuine interest in the position offered.

Is the candidate really qualified? Thanks to the hundreds of career books on the market, job seekers have become expert at tailoring themselves for the opportunity at hand. A good cover letter provides real evidence that its writer has enough skills or experience to apply for the job.

Best Tip

Look for clear thinking in cover letters. Good, simple, forceful writing comes only from an organized mind.

What does the candidate know about your organization? Good candidates will familiarize themselves with your organization and let you know, in the cover letter, that they've done their homework.

Does the letter show clear thinking? Good writers are clear thinkers who can express themselves simply. These are the kind of people you want in your organization.

Does the letter show business sense? Your best candidates know that despite all the idealistic posturing in business publications and corporate PR statements, business is about making a profit. That comes before good deeds like donating money or employing the homeless. Look for a numbers orientation or a focus on the customer. These are the people who will work efficiently on your behalf.

Reject any candidate who sends you a cover letter or résumé that contains spelling or grammatical errors.

Are there typographical or grammatical errors? Anyone who sends out a cover letter with errors in it doesn't deserve a minute of your time.

Has the person done a good sales job? A good sales job in a cover letter makes you want to interview the person. The candidate uses just the right words or phrases—perhaps echoing the qualifications asked for in the ad—or outlines experience and skills in a way that intrigue you. Better, she talks in terms of benefits to you. This is good. You want people who can sell themselves and who understand how they can satisfy one of your important needs.

Next: Scan Résumés

Be aware that anywhere between 20 and 50 percent of all résumés contain lies. These may be outright lies, like jobs never held or degrees never earned. Or they may be half lies, as when a person claims full responsibility for a success that involved other people.

It's hard to spot lies at this stage; that's more easily done when interviewing or checking references.

Here's what to look for in résumés:

The chronological vs. the functional résumé. Chronological résumés are those we're used to—they list jobs held in order by date. Functional résumés group by skills and abilities.

People with spotty job records, or those who have been out of the workforce for a while, are sometimes forced to use the functional method. A chronological résumé would prompt too many questions.

Best Tip

Look for genuine accomplishments—especially those that relate directly to the achievement factors you identified.

Don't hold a functional résumé against a person. Maybe he or she took time out to raise children, or spent five years working as a rock star, circus clown, or chef. The time not spent at a traditional job may have been well spent—for both of you.

Gaps. Explore, in interviews, all time gaps. Don't hold a gap against a person.

Accomplishments. This is the most important item. Look for rock-hard accomplishments in the résumé, preferably in the form of numbers ("increased sales by $750,000"). If the person is a good candidate, you'll find such nuggets. These include accomplishments that resulted in things like:

- New sales
- Productivity and efficiency improvements
- Successful programs initiated
- Successful new products or services
- Profit improvement
- Cost cutting.

In the interview, you'll want to find out the how, where, and when of the accomplishments, as well as to what extent the person was responsible for results.

Errors. As in the cover letter, watch for typographical errors, ungrammatical constructions, fuzzy thinking, and poor judgment. Any of these things on a résumé are large, red flags.

One last thing—I always look at the postmark on the envelope that contains the résumé. I consider it a bad sign if senders used their current company's postage machine to send it. It's a small theft, to be sure. But it's one that could indicate the potential for larger thefts. It may also signal a sense of entitlement—someone who thinks it's perfectly all right to use the company's resources for personal things.

Evaluating cover letters usually knocks about a third of the people out of the running. Scanning résumés will knock another third out. The last third are those you'll want to investigate further before setting up an interview. (Don't throw out the "maybes"—you may need to go over résumés again if your search turns up only a few suitable candidates.)

Cull the Best; Screen by Phone

Your search should yield five to ten good possibilities for a job.

Once you have that many, get on the phone. Phone interviews will help you shorten your list of interviewees to three to five.

Use phone interviews to:

- Test for genuine interest in the position and company;
- Screen for additional fitness for the position;
- Ask for samples or more information;
- Make sure the person knows what's involved;
- Make sure the money is right.

Use the phone interview to get a sense of the person. First talk about the position, and ask preliminary questions about what he or she does at the current job (or did). Gather information and sift it as you converse. A good sign: the person asks good, pointed questions about the job and company. Hiring well is a two-way street—it's best to give candidates as much information as you can. They may find reasons to disqualify themselves, saving you both time.

For this reason, I always talk about money in a phone interview: "The job pays between $30,000 and $35,000. Is that in the ballpark for you?" Some people will disqualify themselves immediately: "I thought it would be higher. I really need something that pays about $10,000 more." "Sorry," you say. "That's what it pays."

It's better, I believe, to prick holes in inflated expectations here than at the end of an in-person interview. It's more awkward then.

If you like what you hear, set up an in-person interview.

What If No One Qualifies?

Never forget: It's better not to hire at all than to hire a mediocre (or worse) candidate. If no one qualifies, begin searching again.

Go back and reread the last chapter. Try a different search method. Talk to new people. Advertise in a different publication. Consider using an agency. Dig deeper.

The Agile Manager's Checklist

✔ Use the job's achievement factors to screen candidates at all stages of the hiring process.

✔ Heed well the wisdom of Robert Half: "A résumé is a balance sheet without any liabilities."

✔ Look for an understanding of the job and your company.

✔ Use phone interviews to weed out candidates who look good only on paper or whose salary expectations are too high.

Interview, Assess, and Choose

"To interview effectively, you must be able to listen effectively."

ROBERT HALF IN *HALF ON HIRING*

Chapter Seven

Assess Yourself

"Did you set up interviews with the candidates yet?" asked Wanda.

"Yes. I'm going to do a lengthy phone interview with the guy from Cincinnati first—I don't want to bring him all the way here if he's not right for the job."

"Are you doing all the interviews yourself?" asked Wanda.

"Your tone tells me that I better not say 'yes.'" Even though he was her boss, he encouraged Wanda to question him. "Why shouldn't I?"

"Well," said Wanda, "for one thing, it's Phil, Anita, and William who are going to be working closely with the new person."

"I'm sorry, Wanda. I'm ultimately responsible for the success of this department, and the best way I know to do that is by making sure every person in it is top-notch. However, I'll let those three have a crack at the top two or three choices."

"Now," said the Agile Manager. "What's the other thing?"

"When we interviewed for Anita's job, a couple of the interviews didn't go well."

"I remember."

"Part of the problem, I think, is the way you come across. When you have a serious task in front of you, you turn on your 'serious

*button.' That scares some people—people who are already ner-
vous to begin with." She gazed directly at the Agile Manager.*

*She'll make a fine boss one day, he thought. "Thank you for
being blunt. You know I appreciate it," he said truthfully. "You were
there—why didn't you step in and throw a few new spices into the
pot?"*

"I didn't know if it was appropriate. May I next time?"

"I'll expect you to."

Before you start meeting people, take stock of yourself. Your
attitude and demeanor will go a long way toward determining whether
you get enough good information to make a hiring decision.

This chapter outlines some pitfalls residing not in the candidates or in the process, but in you, the interviewer. Some of the
items are meant to challenge you to be your best. Sometimes
that means stepping aside and letting another handle interviews,
and sometimes that means questioning your motives in hiring
less-than-stellar people.

Empathize

Empathetic people get the most and the best information in
interviews. Empathy is the ability to put yourself in another's
shoes. It doesn't mean you agree with the person or even like him.
It means you can begin to understand why he is the way he is.

Truly empathetic people are rare. The main reason: It's hard for
most people to get outside of themselves—their roles, concerns,
beliefs, aspirations, and upbringing—to meet others on their home turf. Nonetheless, it's a skill
you can develop with practice.

When you're empathetic, you're able to put people at ease
quickly. The more relaxed candidates are, the better the quality

> **Best Tip**
>
> To get the best information about a person, empathize. It's a skills you can develop with practice.

of information you'll get. That's important, because you don't have much time to get to know a person in an interview.

If you're not empathetic, consider letting a colleague interview with you and do at least some of the talking.

Know Yourself

Are you aloof? Gregarious? Reserved? A real "people" person? Whatever personality type you are, you'll tend to favor those sharing your primary traits.

Sometimes this is good. You're outgoing and like to laugh, for instance, and you're hiring for a hospitality position. You want people who like to laugh and talk, so your personality is perfect for attracting the like-minded.

Other times you work against yourself. You're the outgoing/laughing type hiring for a cloistered, accounting position. You may dismiss out of hand a good-but-serious bean counter, someone who could contribute.

It doesn't matter what kind of person you are. Just know that your personality will, to a large extent, shape the interview. Empathy, again, helps you get inside people and mirror their personality instead. That relaxes them, and it allows you to recognize their good points.

Are You Threatened by Good People?

Many managers hire the mediocre, because they fear strong people.

They think a strong person will make them look bad or upstage them. They think a strong person will earn the loyalty of others in the department. They think a strong person will end up in their job.

Hiring weak people makes you mediocre. Staffed with merely fair people, your department or company can't excel. In hiring weak people, you hurt yourself the most.

Just something to keep in mind.

'I'm a Great Judge of People'

For some reason, a lot of managers feel they are good judges of human character. Even after a string of bad hires. I guess we all have a desire to think of ourselves as wise.

This book gives you the tools to improve your batting average in hiring considerably. But all these tools are wasted if you get to the interview stage and fall into an old, bad habit—hiring on instinct.

Really good judges of character are few and far between. And they back up their instincts with facts and analysis. Use your intuition to augment and support the factual information you get from an interview.

Muzzle Yourself

Many hiring managers have a tough time keeping their mouths shut during interviews. Watch out. The more you talk, the less you learn about the person in front of you.

Best Tip

Don't express your point of view on anything. A smart candidate will feed the view back to you to please you.

Also, beware of expressing your point of view. You don't want to give interviewees any indication of the kinds of answers you're looking for. If you state your opinion on a few matters, the candidate will pick up on what pleases you and be sure to wend it into the conversation.

Best bet: Seem to be interested in everything the candidate has to say, and seem to agree with all the answers, even if contradictory.

Put Your Biases Aside?

Every hiring expert says, "Put your biases aside when interviewing. Keep an open mind." Good advice—for a saint.

Biases—values and beliefs—are all we are. We couldn't put aside our biases aside if we tried. There'd be nothing left.

But you can understand what your biases are. Some of these came out in the job description and success factors you wrote— "need energetic person," "self-starter," "profit-minded," and so forth.

Other biases you may hide even from yourself: *I prefer female candidates, I won't hire anyone without Fortune 100 work experience, I want an Ivy-Leaguer, I'd like a Southerner, No way I'm hiring one of those twentysomething slackers, I already like this guy who went to Notre Dame.*

Beware your biases. You can't avoid having them, but you can at least know what they are.

Be aware of your biases, and fight the worst of them (especially anything having to do with race, creed, or color). Businesses stumble when filled with clones—people who all went to similar school or had the same kind of work experience.

The best way to fight your biases? Keep your hiring criteria clear, and focus on a candidate's accomplishments.

The Agile Manager's Checklist

✔ Understand that whatever your personality type, you'll favor those candidates that match it. This can work for you or against you, depending on the position.

✔ If you've been hiring mediocre workers, look yourself in the mirror and ask, "Am I afraid of strong people?"

✔ Most people are *not* good judges of character.

✔ Be aware of your biases, and fight the worst of them.

Chapter Eight

Create an Interview Strategy

"OK, Wanda," said the Agile Manager. "We've got four interviews tomorrow and four on Thursday. We've identified the most important qualifications and we've got a list of preliminary questions. I'm thinking maybe we should plan to give our top prospects a little test."

"What do you have in mind? And when?" asked Wanda blandly. She often thought he was a bit too careful at times. It slowed things down.

"After we've figured out who the finalists are. We give the person one of our simple products. We ask her—him, I mean—to write a one-paragraph product description and a one-page description of how to use just one feature. Then they import what they've written into a desktop publishing program and design it."

"Come on—how can we expect them to learn our program on the spot?"

"There's a workstation in marketing that Phil says has every graphics program known to humanity on it. They can do the work there, using a program they know."

"Don't you think that's a little tough? How can they know what the 2800 does?" Wanda pursed her lips.

"Of course it's tough. That's the point. A test separates the wheat from the chaff. Besides, we can tell 'em they can make up a feature and what it does. I just want to make sure they can write under pressure and pump out a basic, acceptable design quickly. That's what the job's all about." The Agile Manager leaned forward and continued. "Besides, Wanda, I think you'll agree that we rushed through the last hire. Though we haven't yet spoken of it, I'm beginning to suspect Brad's not working out. Or we have to restructure his job."

Wanda sighed. "I know. Anita and I were just talking about him. OK, so let's test. And take our time."

Your main goal in an interview is to get information that shows whether the candidate has the achievement factors you've identified.

Secondary goals include judging the person's chemistry with you and others in your work group, as well as selling the position and your company. You'll have other goals depending on your situation.

You need a game plan to reach your goals. "Winging" an interview frequently results in failure.

There Is No Recipe

Each interview for each position is different, depending on the position, the person applying for it, you, your company, and your industry. Also, your line of questioning may change if the interview takes an unusual or interesting turn. You may find yourself traveling down a road you hadn't anticipated.

Further, your most important questions deal with learning about a candidate's specific accomplishments—what he did and when, how he did it and why.

That's why there are no universal recipes for a successful job interview. You have to whip up a set of questions from scratch based on what you have in the larder. Your list of achievement factors will guide you, but the questions you ask, and the order you ask them, are up to you.

Ask the Right Questions

To get good information, ask good questions. Starting on page 60, you'll find sample questions to spark your thinking. Many can be followed up with a simple request to keep the interviewee talking: "Tell me more."

Back in chapter three, you created a worksheet like the one on the facing page. (If you didn't, do it now. Feel free to enlarge this one on a copier.) Keeping that page in front of you, create questions designed to help you know whether the person in front of you has the qualities and qualifications you need.

The achievement factors will prompt a mixed bag of questions that concern:

- Facts
- Work history and experience
- Skills and abilities
- Work ethic and values
- Intelligence and aptitude
- Personal characteristics.

Some questions yield answers in more than one area. For example: "What did you do each day?" (Work ethic, experience, skills.) "Did you like your boss? Why not?" (Values, intelligence.)

Using the example of the aerospace industry securities analyst, let's create just a few probable questions.

Facts: What were your grades in college? What degrees have you earned? What training have you received in your area since college? Do you have a valid securities license? Are you able to travel five to seven days out of the month? What was your title in the last job? How many people did you supervise? Did you set the department's budget?

Experience and work history: Tell me about your jobs, beginning with Fuller Investment Advisors. Considering your engineering degree, why didn't you go straight into industry? Did you start out as an aerospace analyst? Your résumé says that in your next job, at Boeing, you helped design the fuselage for the

Achievement Factors/Interviewing Notes

Date:
Job:
Candidate:

Achievement Factors:	Yes	No
1._____	___	___
2._____	___	___
3._____	___	___
4._____	___	___
5._____	___	___
6._____	___	___
7._____	___	___
8._____	___	___
9._____	___	___
10._____	___	___

Comments:_____

_____
_____
_____
_____
_____
_____
_____
_____

Sample Interview Questions

Have you ever been convicted of a crime?

Why do you want to change jobs?

Tell me, in detail, what a typical day is like for you. How about a tough day?

What do you like to do outside of work?

Do you like to work with ideas or numbers?

What are your basic, core values?

Did you like school? Which subjects did you like best?

To communicate an idea to a number of people, would your rather give a presentation, or write a report or memo?

Tell me about your first job.

Who are your heroes? Tell me about one.

Where do you want to be in, say, three years.

Where would you like to be in ten years?

Do you like your present employer? Why or why not?

Would you rather have a modest salary with the chance for a big performance-based bonus, or would you rather have a larger salary with no chance for a bonus?

Do you like to play sports?

Are you happy with how fast you've come in your career?

Do you like routine?

How do you deal with stress?

Of all the things you do now on your present job, which do you like the best? The least?

What are your professional goals?

Can you switch gears easily? Give me an example.

Do you like to initiate action? Tell me of a time you did.

Now that you've heard about the job, what would you change in it to make it a perfect fit for you?

What outside-the-job activities are you involved in?

Do you get bored easily?

How do you feel about the possibility of moving to a large [small] organization?

767. What was your exact role in that? Why did you decide to go back to the securities industry? Did you get fired? When did you move over to Wagner & Associates?

Skills and abilities: Have you ever given a presentation? How many? Tell me about an industry research project you conducted. How did you gather information? How did you arrive at your conclusion? Name a security you recommended that earned its buyers a nice return. Name one you recommended that didn't pan out. Why didn't it? What did you learn from that failure? Did you win any sales awards? Tell me about a time you had a problem with an employee at work. How did you resolve it?

Best Tip

Come up with questions that reveal demonstrated accomplishment in specific areas.

Work ethic and values: Did you like your boss at Wagner? Why not? What did you do all day? How many hours did you work each day? How do you relax? How did you respond when your sales manager tried to get you to move a block of securities before, say, the end of the day? Did you ever see another broker churn an account? What did you do? Who is your hero in the industry? Why? Where do you want to be in, say, five years?

Intelligence/aptitude: If you had been in charge of your department at Fuller, what would you have done differently? Where do you see the investment industry headed in the next few years? Do you think we need more regulation? Why? How do you stay up with current aerospace industry practices? What do you think about all the industry mergers that have been going on?

Personal characteristics: When institutional investors called on you for advice, was it easy to take a stand? Tell me about a specific time you did that. Tell me about your speech at the '97 convention. What did it feel like speaking to 2,500 people? Have you ever been passed over for a promotion you wanted? How did you handle it? What do you like to do in your spare time? How do you motivate people to do good work?

Why are you changing careers?

Are you prepared to travel overnight two weeks out of the month?

Run down your salary history for me.

Ever had two jobs at once? Tell me how you juggled them.

What were you doing during [whatever gaps are on the résumé]?

Would you rather be out in the field or at your desk? Why?

What are your best strengths? Tell me how you've used a couple of them on the job.

What are your weaknesses?

Tell me about the last crisis you faced. What did you do?

Describe a problem you've recently encountered and how you dealt with it.

Why should we hire you?

Tell me about a lousy boss you had and how you dealt with him or her.

What unique value can you offer us?

Tell me about a failure or something that didn't turn out as you expected.

Tell me about a couple of your recent major accomplishments. What were they, and how did you succeed? What kind of help did you have?

Have you developed new skills lately? What are they?

Which of your skills and abilities will make you succeed in this position?

How do you stay organized?

What did your [former] employers not like about you?

If you were your present boss, how would you have run the department differently?

What do you think you're really good at?

Were you fired? Why?

Give me an example of how you made a tough decision.

Tell me about a problem you had with a peer and how you resolved it.

Most of these questions require something other than a one or two word response. These questions get people talking, which is when you'll learn the most.

Create Hypothetical Scenarios

One good way to understand candidates is to put them in a hypothetical problem situation. Examples:

"You've just locked the door and a customer comes up and starts knocking on it. You have to pick up your child at day care in ten minutes. What do you do?"

"You answer the phone, and there's a customer literally screaming at you about a lost shipment. What do you do?"

"Your best employee just told you she's taking a job elsewhere, and she can give you only one week's notice. What do you do?"

"A vendor tells you that one of your buyers tried to shake him down for a weekend in the country in exchange for a large order. What do you do?"

The Psychological Aspect of Hiring

Ask a few questions to help you understand the psychological underpinnings of the person you're interviewing.

Executive recruiter John Wareham—author of the superb *Secrets of a Corporate Headhunter*—believes psychology is just about everything. He makes it a point to find out:

- What kind of upbringing the candidate had
- The role the person's father and mother played
- The values the candidate holds
- The person's present non-job circumstances (home life, family, etc.).

Wareham wants to know, for instance, what kind of father a candidate had or has. Was he a hard-driving person? Absent? What values did he instill in his son or daughter?

A woman born on the "wrong side of the tracks" for instance,

How many people do [did] you manage?

How much time do you spend thinking, planning?

Are you a delegator? Give me an example.

Do you like meetings? How do you make them effective?

Have you had good luck hiring people?

Can you read financial statements? What do you look for?

Has any of your people gone on to better things?

Describe your favorite boss.

What is your opinion on [something related to the field]?

Is your company too bureaucratic?

In what ways have the departments you've overseen improved?

How do you motivate people to do good work?

Do you have budget responsibility?

Have you had profit-and-loss responsibility?

Beyond skills, what are your abilities (good with numbers, languages, able to manipulate software, etc.)?

Ever had to fire someone? How did you do it?

Do your subordinates consider you a friend?

Do you like to be in charge?

Do you like to sell?

Do you set policy or strategy, or do you administer it?

Do you do the same work your people do? Because you have to or because you want to?

How do you get along with your peers?

How long have you been in this field?

What excites you about it?

Ask questions that show the candidate can come up with solutions to technical problems (like those involving formulas, systems, processes, etc.).

What software programs are you familiar with?

Ask questions that show knowledge of important job-related regulations (postal, environmental, etc.).

Where do you think the industry is headed in the next few years?

may—thirty years of successes later—still feel she has something to prove. That motivation works in your favor. Or a man with a hard-driving father may still be trying to live up to his father's ambitions for him—years after the father's death.

Wareham believes it's knowledge like this, along with demonstrated accomplishment, that best predicts a person's job performance.

If nothing else, keep in mind two clichés: *Past is prologue,* and *The apple doesn't fall far from the tree.*

Pre-Interview Considerations

Here are a few things to think about after you've formulated questions but before you meet candidates:

Don't plan to interview all day. You may be tempted to see everyone all in one day to get the task over with. If you do, you'll exhaust yourself by the end of the day—and pity the poor candidate who can't seem to hold your attention.

Also, keep interviews to an hour or less (except for second or third interviews for important jobs). You can always see a candidate again.

Arrange seating to relax people. If you sit behind a desk with the candidate on the other side, you'll send a message: "I'm more powerful than you, and you better not forget it." Sometimes, though rarely, this is the message you want to send.

Move away from desks and sit face to face or side by side with nothing in between. Doing so puts people at ease. If more than two people are present, arrange chairs in a circle.

Plan to judge everyone by the same criteria. Everyone deserves a chance. Don't relax your standards on an achievement factor unless you're getting a qualification of major importance in return.

Judging everyone based on the form you created is also a good way to show you hired without breaking discrimination laws.

Consider doing the interview "backwards." Rather than describe the job first and then ask questions, do the reverse. That way candidates can't tailor responses to make their skills seem to fit the job perfectly.

Don't be influenced by personality or credentials. If you must, repeat this mantra before each interview: "Accomplishment, accomplishment, accomplishment . . ." If you find yourself liking a person in advance based on a résumé and phone interview, become your own devil's advocate. Start with the assumption that "there must be something wrong with this person. I'll find out what it is in the interview."

Questions about national origin. In two words: Don't ask. That includes seemingly innocuous questions like, "Are you legally permitted to work here?" Though technically OK to ask a question like that, an employment lawyer tells me it raises red flags. He says it's best to wait until a potential employee has to fill out forms like the W-2 to make sure a person can work in the U.S. You run the risk of deciding upon a candidate you can't hire, but it saves you from a potential discrimination lawsuit.

Fill out forms immediately after each interview. Keep facts fresh in your mind. If you interview more than five people or so, you'll have trouble remembering what the first person looks like, let alone what her best qualities are.

The form on page 59 has a space for comments at the bottom. Use it to put your general impressions, as well as any other item you care to remember. If you're interviewing a lot of people, be sure to write down a few characteristics to jog your memory. ("Red hair and beard." "Spoke very fast, seemed nervous.")

More than One Interview?

Everyone hired at Cypress Semiconductor goes through four to six interviews.

That might seem excessive to some, but think about what's at stake. Hiring a person is like a marriage, considering the time you'll spend with the person and the legal hurdles in place to prevent an easy severing of the relationship.

Would you marry someone after just one date? That's exactly

what you do when you meet a person once and offer a job.

Here are a few of the reasons you might want to meet a person more than once:

1. You have more questions prompted by answers the candidate gave in the first interview.
2. You want people whom the finalist will be working with to meet, get to know, and approve of him.
3. You need to test for skills, abilities, or fortitude. Tests may range from a typing test to having the person solve a technical problem or give a presentation.
4. Your boss wants a session with whomever you wish to hire.
5. You have nagging doubts about a candidate and want to keep meeting until you uncover the source of your concerns.
6. Your team system demands a "peer" interview in which the team has veto power over a hire.
7. You were astonished by the candidate's brilliance in the first interview, and you want to make sure it's real.
8. After checking references, you have new concerns.

Some people say, "You'd better snap up a good person right away or someone else will." That happens, but rarely. In my view, it's riskier to leap before you've spent enough time looking.

Block out enough time to meet a finalist two or maybe three times, plus a couple of phone chats. For lower level positions, meet at least twice—and test.

The Agile Manager's Checklist

✔ Take time to formulate penetrating questions—those that reveal whether candidates have the achievement factors.

✔ Your questions should cover experience, skills, values, intelligence, and desirable personal characteristics.

✔ When in doubt, interview again.

Chapter Nine

Interview (and Assess)

". . . I've done about thirteen projects for them," he said, handing a copy of a manual to both Wanda and the Agile Manager.

The Agile Manager took his without looking at it. "Thanks. Mind if I keep it for a few days?"

"Not at all."

"Good," he continued. "Now about your work for Standard. You only did one project for them. Why not more?"

The candidate seemed eager to respond. "My contact there took a job with another company immediately after that project. She started giving me more work, and I never had reason to go back to Standard."

Wanda and the Agile Manager had spent a good half hour looking for weak points. They'd found a few minor items—one missed deadline, a dissatisfied customer, but not much more. Pretty good so far, thought Wanda. She said, "Why do you want a regular job after free-lancing for five years?"

"I work about sixty hours a week. Only half of that is billable . . ."

Wanda quickly did some calculations in her head—he said he charged $30 an hour. That's $900 a week. Take away a third for taxes, another $100 for overhead, and he's left with $500 take home. Good. We're in the ball park.

". . . so I figure I spend at least fifteen hours a week chasing down work, connecting with people, fiddling around with projects in ways I don't feel I can bill for—"

"What do you mean?" asked Wanda.

"Oh, I do things like wake up in the middle of the night thinking, 'Maybe I should have used Bodoni for the subheads instead of Caslon,' so I get up and mess around in Quark. Before I know it, it's time for breakfast." The candidate smiled, knowing he'd scored a number of points with that one.

This is looking good, thought Wanda. But when I'm done checking references, I'll know more about him than his mother.

You've got a strategy, you've got questions, and you've got a candidate arriving in ten minutes. What do you do?

First, take a few minutes to review the résumé. Remind yourself of its inconsistencies, weaknesses, strengths, and oddities. You'll want to investigate each one, in addition to asking the questions you'll ask of everyone you meet.

Then remind yourself of your task: to find someone willing and able to do the job.

Best Tip

Just before the interview, scan the résumé one last time. Look for real accomplishment in areas of importance to you

Also, scan the following list to remind you what constitutes accomplishment. It'll keep you from being blinded by a good personality or impressive credentials. Look for:

- Sales increased, costs cut
- New, successful programs installed/initiated
- Major enhancements to the organization added (like created a Web site or developed a side business)
- Productivity improved
- Entrepreneurial thinking paid off
- Number of customers increased
- Processes improved

- Quality, customer service, inventory turns, collection period, etc., improved
- A new product/service successfully launched
- Business overseas or a new market opened up.

Begin Lightly

When the interviewee comes in, make her feel at home. Stand up, look her in the eye, greet her warmly, invite her to sit down, and talk briefly about some idle topic like the weather. Thank her for coming in to hear about the job, then start talking about it or the company. If you're doing the interview "backwards" (see page 65), say something like, "We're going to do this interview a little bit differently than others you've probably had. We'll start with some questions about your jobs and skills, then talk about the position here."

Take a few minutes to put the candidate at ease by making small talk—but begin assessing the person immediately.

Begin getting useful information with some easy factual questions, then probe work history and, perhaps, education. Start easy, then ask progressively more difficult or involved questions as time goes on. And be ready to switch gears or change your game plan if the situation warrants it. (But always with the aim of assessing the primary qualifications you seek.)

Keep your list of questions and achievement factors before you at all times. I put them on a clipboard and make notes as I talk.

Begin Assessing Immediately

Assessing candidates begins the moment they walk through the door. It doesn't end until you've decided they are or aren't right for the job. That can take more than one interview.

The achievement factors are the most important items to assess. But you have many other things to appraise, too—personality characteristics, interpersonal skills, original thinking, and overall intelligence, to name a few.

Starting on page 73, you'll find things to look for that will help you assess the candidate during and after the interview. Take note of those that apply to the position you're interviewing for, and make sure you ask some questions that shed light on the item.

An Expert Interviewer's Checklist

People will be forthcoming with real accomplishments and things they feel good about or know in detail. They'll be less forthcoming about skills or abilities they feel they lack. And they'll stonewall you about things they've lied or misled you about.

It's absolutely necessary to probe for the qualities—or lack of them—you need on the job. The following tips will help you uncover strengths or deficiencies:

Watch for inconsistencies. Liars or tellers of half-truths sometimes say contradictory things in interviews. "I headed the project team that developed the SuperChocolateSupreme," he'll say at the beginning of the interview. "We were a team of peers at Company X" he'll say later. "Whoa," you say, "I thought you managed the team?" "Well, I guess I was more of a facilitator," he admits—and you've learned a few important things about his work history and his character.

Watch body language. Everyone speaks with their bodies as well as with their voices. If people aren't telling the truth or the whole truth, their bodies will say one thing while their words say another. "Yes, I did graduate cum laude," he says while looking downward briefly. "No, I got along fine with everyone in my department," she says while quickly folding her arms across her chest.

Follow up with questions whenever you harbor a doubt. "You never had a problem with anyone in your department?" you ask with raised eyebrows.

The point is not to expose the person before you as a fraud. Follow up as much as you need to until you're reasonably certain you're not getting the truth, then change subjects. Keep your opinions to yourself.

Probe weak spots. Everyone you meet will present a solid front. One of your jobs is to probe for weak spots. If weak spots are isolated, and you can live with them, fine. But weak spots sometimes indicate extensive dry rot.

You'll often know when you hit a weak spot through body language. You'll see a flash in the eye, an involuntary wince, or a quick change of subject. People are especially sensitive about jobs that didn't go well, and what they may consider a lack of educational or other qualifications.

Get more information, but only when it's important to do so. Your focus should be anchored to performance in the job at hand. For example:

"So you were called a designer, but you didn't do much drafting?"

"Not really."

"Why not?"

"I sketched the product in Freehand, or sometimes on paper. We had a person to do the scut work."

"So you don't know any CAD software?"

"I used a program occasionally."

"Which one?"

"I, uh, can't remember the name. It was on the network."

"I see."

The trick is to ask pointed questions without tormenting the candidate. You want answers, not to show who's boss. Besides, it's not necessary to torment people with job-disqualifying weaknesses; they'll do it to themselves.

Keep the conversation going. To keep the candidate talking, resort to comments like,

"Tell me more about it."

"And then what happened?"

"How did she react to that?"

"What did you do?"

"Why?"

"How so?"

Silence, too, is a great way to keep people talking. Especially

Assessment Factors

Most important are the achievement factors you've identified as essential for the job you have available. You should put most of your effort into questions that provide information on them. Other things to look for:

Enthusiasm. As Robert Half says, when in doubt, hire the most enthusiastic candidate.

Interest in job and company.

Interest in you and others in the work group.

An "entitlement" attitude. Some people believe the world owes them a living—and a good one. They are the first to walk off with pens, use the phone for personal long-distance calls, and clamor for more money and benefits. Avoid them.

Appropriate dress and grooming.

Politeness. Ask anyone who came into contact with the candidate for a reaction. She might have been sugary sweet with you while treating your secretary like dirt.

Criticizes former employers. One of my biggest hiring mistakes ever could have been averted. To rationalize a string of bad jobs, a candidate had convinced himself he'd been wronged at every turn by spiteful bosses. His tale of woe began in the interview. I believed him and even thought of myself in heroic terms for rescuing this poor man. It didn't take me long to discover why no one could tolerate him.

Something to prove or some other inner motivation to succeed. Sometimes you can feel it, other times you have to uncover it. When you find it, hire it.

Overqualified. Will she be bored in a job beneath her or one without opportunities for growth? Some experts recommend hiring overqualified workers nearing retirement. It can be a bargain.

when they'd rather not. Most people will rush to fill in the silence—sometimes with very revealing information.

Challenge statements made or résumé items. At times, you'll need to put the candidate on the spot. Maybe you don't believe the statement 100 percent, or maybe you just want quick confirmation of something you have no reason to doubt. For example, "You say you had profit-and-loss responsibility in your job at Acme. Can you give me the name of somebody who will confirm that for me?" Or, "Can I see the transcript for your years at the University of Minnesota?"

Look for the right attitude and appearance. Don't neglect information you gather without asking questions.

Southwest Airlines, for example, looks for friendly, smiling, humorous people. The evidence for that can be found without questioning.

Also, many high-level jobs have an important symbolic component: Does she look like a leader? Does he dress, act, and have the right presence to deal with wealthy clients? Will people believe her in the role of an expert?

Fend Off Professional Candidates

Since the career "industry" has sprung up, it's harder to hire well. Too many people know too many tricks to divert the attention of the unwary interviewer, to hide weaknesses, and to appear to be what they are not.

I fault some books with their "anything goes" attitude. The message: "Considering the tough job market, anything you can do to get a job is permissible." Don't do anything illegal, such books say, but take control of the process early. (Actually, one book I consulted recently told of a job seeker who lied about his age by doctoring all the dates on his résumé. The book faulted him not for lying but for not committing all the dates to memory for the interview, where he was exposed.)

What ever happened to simply being good at something, compiling a record of accomplishment, and working to find the right

Industry. You'll see this in a prodigious output—of things or useful ideas.

Contributor. This is the mark of the person who has improved the organization everywhere she has worked. Hire her.

Judgment. Best uncovered by asking "what if" questions.

A grasp of what your company does and how he can contribute.

Energy. This manifests itself in different ways. It may be visible to all, or it may be reflected in the level of output.

Can think on his feet. Seen in answering difficult questions or those with no right answer.

Stability in jobs, family, etc. Stability is a character trait, and a desirable one for most jobs.

Curiosity. The curious learn more and faster than others. (They are also easily diverted from more important things.)

Achievement orientation. Some people like to collect achievements—things they can point to with pride. The more you have such people on your staff, the better you look. These people like to chew through tasks. And they take the time to complete what they begin.

Power orientation. Some people crave power over things and others. This isn't necessarily a bad thing. Most leaders crave power. In the best cases, they learn the human relations skills and maintain the ethical standards that allow them to use it wisely.

Firm handshake. I'll never hire anyone, man or woman, who gives me a dead-fish handshake (barring disability).

Short attention span. You'll see this in an inability to develop an answer to a complicated question and in eyes quickly darting around the office at the wrong time. Not usually good for an organization.

situation to excel? What does anyone gain by getting an ill-suited job through subterfuge?

Most career books counsel job seekers to arrive at the interview with their own strategy—to highlight certain accomplishments, downplay others, and hide embarrassing facts any way possible.

If any job seeker is successful in working a strategy at the expense of your own, you've lost. You've lost twice if you go on to hire that person.

Knowledge is power. Watch for these tricks:

The candidate seeks to interview you. "Boy, your job must be interesting. How many people do you supervise?" I'm all for giving a prospect all the information needed about a job, working conditions, people, and the company—at the proper time. But some candidates will ask you questions to divert attention from their own record (or lack of it). Make sure candidates do most of the talking in interviews (at least 80 percent).

Don't let candidates take control of the interview. If they do, they'll work their strategy while you sit and twitch.

The candidate brings up items on his or her agenda, not yours. This is another diversionary tactic or an attempt to keep your attention on particular strengths. For example, you ask, "What has been your major accomplishment at United in the past year?" "I've done a lot in the past year," the candidate answers, "project teams and committee work mostly. Three years ago I really hit a home run with the service department overhaul. What I did then was to . . ."

"I'll get to that," you break in. "I want to know about this year's accomplishments."

The candidate talks a lot without saying anything. You've encountered the kind of person who talks a great game but produces little. These people are often great interviewees. Good communicators, they talk about being in on this and that, on

Customer focus. Those with a bureaucratic temperament care more about systems and processes inside a company. That's deadly these days. Hire those who look outward to those the company serves.

Able to make mistakes and carry on. A (short) history of mistakes in a candidate can be good—it shows the willingness to take risks. No risk takers, no growth for a company.

Able to handle change. More important these days.

Can work in teams. People with healthy egos and ambition can stand time spent in teams, as long as work offers opportunities to shine.

Entrepreneurial. Not appropriate for every job. On the other hand, why shouldn't everyone be thinking about how the organization can make an extra buck?

Interrupts you. Not good.

Mature (emotionally as well as intellectually). The emotionally mature think of others beyond themselves and can sacrifice.

Procrastination. Evidence: Projects not completed, little output for years worked.

Looks you in the eye. Good. Of course, some brazen liars learned early to stare you down as they spout their most outrageous lies.

Starts asking about what's in it for me too soon. You're barely seated when you're asked about salary and benefits. Comp time policy is of more interest than job duties. Danger.

Argumentative. Beware.

Good speaking skills. Snap up articulate people able to make a coherent argument or point (assuming they have a record of accomplishment).

Assertive and self-confident. Good.

Sends a thank-you note. A silver star for those who do. Politeness is a habit that has a positive impact on customers.

knowing important people in the industry, and they use all the latest buzzwords. You're impressed—until you stop to consider what the person has actually accomplished.

Expose such people by keeping the conversation focused on on-the-job successes. "What did you do? When did you do it? How did you do it? What was your role? What were the results?"

The candidate who hides or deflects problems. Follow up, follow up, follow up.

"So the product failed?"

"Well, not exactly. We had to pull it from the market, though."

"So it failed?"

"Not really. It just didn't meet our expectations."

"What were your expectations?"

"We hoped to sell more than we had by that point. But I was against it—I thought things were starting to pick up. It would've been great. I had all kinds of ancillary items planned for it—"

You cut him off, understanding that, yes indeed, it was a failure.

The candidate who rationalizes or turns a negative event into a positive one. Job-hunting books encourage job seekers to have a positive spin ready for any negative. "Even though I did get fired from that job, I learned later that the boss had been under a lot of pressure to meet profit targets. He had to get rid of a few people to cut payroll and meet them. I was the victim, really, of corporate policy." You can either follow up or change the subject, having heard enough.

Talk About the Job in Detail

If you haven't done so at the start of the interview, describe the job in great detail. Explain daily duties, expectations, who the person will work with, who is the boss, the nature of any team work. Provide as much detail as necessary and invite questions, both about the job and about the company.

Listen closely for good questions. Nobody can understand the real nature of a job from a five-minute discussion, so I consider it odd if the person doesn't have a few questions.

Inquisitive in the right ways. That is, about the job and how she could succeed in it.

Good listener. Few are. A high-order skill, and especially valuable for customer service or sales positions.

Talks in terms of benefits he/she could provide you. Great!

Good chemistry. Of paramount importance in the executive suite; only slightly less so elsewhere.

On time for the interview or a good reason why not. If he can't make the interview on time . . .

Ethical. She didn't badmouth current employer, nor let on any trade secrets.

Teamwork mentality. Speaks in terms of "we," not "I."

Gets out in the world. Beware the deskbound manager. Good ones visit customers, other departments, or their people regularly.

Needs the money. Good motivator.

Salary, Benefits, Perks

I always save discussion about salary until the end. In part that's because I've noted the salary range in the phone interview. The other reason is that I want the candidate to understand the job in detail. That's good information they can use to put the salary in perspective.

Watch carefully the candidate's face as you provide numbers. It'll give you advance warning about the candidate's expectations.

Also, this is the time for the candidate to say, "All of this sounds really good to me. I'm very interested in the job. But I have to be honest and tell you that it's about $5,000 less than I'm making now, and I wouldn't be likely to take it if offered at that salary."

A good candidate will then go on to explain the value he or she can provide you, justifying an increased salary.

You just got good information. Use it. Maybe it knocks the candidate out of contention, or maybe you'll decide to offer this person another $5,000—or more.

End Cordially, Scribble Furiously

When you have enough information, or when time's up, end the interview on a cordial note.

Sometimes you know a person isn't right in the first ten minutes. Don't waste anyone's time—end it. I remember interviewing for a job when I was in college. I used the phrase "summer job," whereupon the interviewer stood up and stuck out his hand, saying, "You just said the unmagic words. Thanks for stopping by."

If you know you need more information from a good candidate, say so. "I may have a few more questions for you. I'll give you a call." If you're sure the candidate is strong enough for another interview or a test, say so: "I'd like you to take a little test sometime next week." If you're not sure about the person, or you need to talk to others first, don't make any promises. "We'll be talking to a few more people this week. Someone will be in touch with you if we'd like to talk to you again."

The Agile Manager's Checklist

✔ Before interviews, scan the job's achievement factors. And remember to look for accomplishment in terms of sales increased, costs cut, processes improved, etc.

✔ In the interview, watch these telltale indicators:

- Inconsistencies;
- Body language;
- Weak areas candidates rush to cover up;
- Accomplishments proclaimed rather too boldly.

✔ Save talk about salary and benefits for the end of the interview.

Chapter Ten

Check References

Wanda, ear glued to the phone and staring at her feet, listened intently to their prime candidate's former boss.

". . . at that point, I just told him to run the operation any way he wanted. He knew a lot more than I did about it, and we all were pleased with the results." Wanda detected genuine warmth in his voice.

"He's been working on his own for five years," said Wanda. "I wonder how well he'd adapt to working in a group and taking direction."

"That could be a concern," said the boss. "He was pretty autonomous here and wanted to be left alone to work. He could get abrasive if someone wanted him to do something over again."

Here's something, thought Wanda. "Do something over? I thought you were pleased with his work."

"Oh, I was very pleased. You see, sometimes a few pieces got sent over to the public relations people. They had different standards. They thought more in terms of 'marketing' than 'information.' So they often wanted a slicker piece where it wasn't warranted. I backed him up a few times on that issue."

Darn. Can't I find anything bad about this guy? "But did he have to work with people a lot?"

"Oh yes. It sounds like your job is much like the one he did for us. He worked with product developers, mostly. And since he wasn't an expert in refrigeration units and heat pumps, he had to discuss products in detail with them to be able to write accurately. He's a good listener. And it showed in his work—people would say they wished every manufacturer's manuals were as clear and simple."

Wanda asked, "Would you mind if I talked to someone at his level—a peer of his?"

"Not at all. . . ."

After a particularly good interview, you may have the urge to extend a job offer without checking references. If there's a bigger mistake you can make as a manager, I can't think of one.

I once hired a person I knew. I also knew the quality of his work. What else do I need to know? I didn't check references.

The result was about twelve months of heartache. Sure, he could do the work—when he wanted to. Checking references would no doubt have tipped me off to a problem with motivation.

The Problem Is, However . . .

Many employers are so afraid of lawsuits by former employees that they will only confirm that a person worked there and perhaps give a title. They won't talk about skills, work ethic, or character.

Best Tip

Never offer a job without checking references. Doing so can create years of pain and remorse.

What are companies afraid of? Violating a raft of federal, state, and local laws concerning privacy. They are especially afraid of managers who may give false or malicious information about a person (with good reason—it's a serious offense). That's why some candidates, knowing that you're likely to have trouble getting good information or that you'll do a less-than-thorough job, make up fictitious information.

Don't prove them right. Jump any hurdle you must to check references.

A rule of thumb: The higher or more critical the position, the more checking you should do. For a job roasting hot dogs, you'll probably just call the last boss. For a job heading a division, you may spend weeks finding out all you can about a prospect.

Most jobs fall in between these two extremes. Talk to at least three people, and maybe five or six. Keep going until you're satisfied that the person has or hasn't got the skills and characteristics you need.

First: Get Permission

Have candidates supply at least three references who can attest to the quality of their work and their overall abilities.

To hold you and those who give you references "harmless" in the eyes of the law, get the candidate's written permission for checking references and factual information regarding certificates, diplomas, or college degrees. Have your lawyer draft the statement. It should include, if possible, permission to check references not supplied by the candidate.

Best Tip

Ask references open-ended questions. For example, "Can you tell me about a time when X made an amazing sale?"

If a candidate won't give you permission, or wants you to stick only to references he or she provides, consider it a red flag.

Your Reference-checking Strategy

As with any other aspect of hiring well, have a plan in mind before you begin checking references. Know whom you want to contact, and what questions you want to ask.

You'll get the best answers using indirect questions. For instance, if you call the references supplied and ask, "Is Jim hard working?" Everyone will say, "Yes!"

Instead, ask a series of questions like, "Can you tell me about a project that Jim took part in that had a stiff deadline? How did he meet it? Was it successful?"

Have a list of questions that will shed light on the qualities and qualifications you're seeking. Ask the most important ones first.

The reason for that: While a few people might be willing to spend all day on the phone with you, most won't. Most people will feel vaguely uncomfortable—in part because of legal considerations, but also because they don't want to say bad things about someone now out of their lives. Be prepared for someone to say, abruptly, "That's all I have time for" and hang up.

With your list of references and questions in hand, proceed in this manner:

1. Check degrees earned. Call the school(s) listed on the résumé and confirm that the person has the credentials claimed.

2. Call references supplied by the candidate. These people will probably be gushing in their praise of the candidate. And they'll be willing to talk longer than the others.

With pointed questions that get references to talk about actual situations, you can glean important information that goes beyond their desire to say good things.

Also, don't be afraid to bring up a known weakness. You can tell a lot by the response. "It appears to me that Jim doesn't really pay attention to detail," you say. Silence. The reference: "Well, uh . . . I'm not sure I'd say that, but he is a real good 'big picture' guy. We depended on him to give us an idea where the industry was headed . . ."

Also, watch for supplied references who aren't overflowing with praise. Not long ago, I was in on hiring a person who seemed to have the right attitude and skills. Two of her three references had nothing but good things to say about her, but the third was not forthcoming and at one point said, "She did the best she could."

> **Best Tip**
>
> If supplied references aren't overflowing with praise, watch out. They may be trying to tell you something.

We hired her. We let her go four months later. Her skills were poor and she could deflect criticism better than anyone I've ever seen. We had no one to blame but ourselves. If a person can't supply three glowing references, there's something wrong.

Another time, a person supplied three references in applying for an important job. One heaped lavish praise, and the other two were, well, bland. And both seemed eager to get off the phone. I heeded their hidden warnings and hired someone else.

Once someone called me about a recent graduate who'd done some free-lance work for me. The person, while doing good work in the end, had a cavalier attitude about work—he'd miss deadlines and meetings, and he acted as if he didn't have to please me.

I pointed all this out to the caller, who proceeded to excuse every fault I mentioned as things "college students do." He wanted, clearly, to hire him. (I wonder how happy he is now.)

3. Call references not supplied. Say a person gives you the name of her most recent boss as a reference, and the name of the boss she had three jobs ago. Call her boss from two jobs ago.

Another way to get new names: Ask the references supplied by the candidate to recommend other people to talk to.

A few tips when calling references:

To get the best information, go as high in the organization as you can. Senior managers know how important it is to get good information about a person before offering a job. They'll spend more time with you and be more forthcoming.

When you call references not given by the candidate, let them know you have permission to do so. And always try to call a specific person. If you call the human resources department, you'll get the "He worked here from 1992 to 1995. That's all I can say" routine.

Don't take all the information you get as gospel. Maybe an old boss has an ax to grind. Or maybe an old boss still feels bad for firing a person, so she disguises that fact and says good things instead. Again, your best bet is to ask questions that show how the person succeeded or used particular skills in concrete situations. "He says he's had lots of experience with AKC software. Did he work with it for you?" "Oh yes, he was our in-house expert. I wish he was still here—it's a bear to work with."

Assess New-found Information

Use the information you get. It may, and probably will, spur new questions in your mind about the person you'd like to hire. These aren't necessarily bad things—you may want more information about skills or experience you hadn't realized the candidate possessed.

Other times you'll want to follow up on a negative. ("A few of your references said you had trouble meeting deadlines. What do you say about that?")

And don't dismiss red flags as "isolated incidents" or "signs of immaturity." Sometimes they will be, other times not.

Occasionally you'll hear things that convince you the person is wrong for the job. Drop him from consideration without hesitation.

The Agile Manager's Checklist

✔ Don't skip reference checking. It's an essential part of the hiring process.

✔ Get permission to check references, including people not on the candidate's list.

✔ When discussing a candidate with a reference, listen to what's being said through tone of voice and enthusiasm.

✔ Don't be afraid to bring up a negative with a reference.

✔ Vow to be as helpful and honest as you can when someone calls you to check out a candidate.

Chapter Eleven

Choose and Make an Offer

The Agile Manager cracked a warm smile. "Well, we did our best, but we couldn't find anyone who would say anything bad about you. And you did great on the test. So we'd like to offer you the job." Wanda and the Agile Manager smiled as the candidate's face lit up.

"As we discussed, the job pays $36,000, with full health insurance for your whole family, educational reimbursement, health club fees paid, life and disability insurance, and a profit-sharing retirement plan. We also have a departmental bonus that we all share— in good years only. You'll report to Wanda, but you'll be working closest with some of the people you met—Anita, William, and Phil. But you know the nature of the job. You'll spend at least half your time glued to the computer."

Wanda added, "The department is growing, and I think you'll have a good opportunity to grow along with it. What do you say?"

"I'll take it! You've made me very happy." The new member of the product-development team tried to stop smiling but couldn't. "And I'm going to do a great job for you!"

We'll see, thought Wanda.

"Great!" said the Agile Manager.

If things have gone according to plan, you have a clear-cut hot prospect. You're ready to make an offer.

You may, however, have more than one good prospect. Here's what to do if you're having trouble choosing. First, it's likely that your prospects aren't good in all the same things. Refer to your list of ranked achievement factors. It'll remind you of the most important qualifications. Compare each candidate on each item, giving preference to the one who comes out on top in the most important categories.

If it's still close, match them on desirable characteristics like congeniality, creativity, or good communication skills.

If it's still close, schedule an additional interview for each. Meet over lunch or in a social situation, where you can observe a different set of skills or characteristics.

If all else fails, arrange a test. One will come out on top.

Before you extend an offer:

Wait a day or two unless you feel you may lose a candidate. Do other things for at least a day, or over the weekend. Don't think about the job or the people who've applied for it. Getting away from the task may provide new insights.

If two candidates are neck and neck, give the nod to the one who shows the most enthusiasm for the job.

Be sure you're choosing without illegal bias. If you've judged everyone by the same criteria, you are, most likely, safe.

Ask yourself: Is this person a lot like me? Beware of hiring clones of yourself. You need diversity of skills and viewpoint.

Check your gut. Now is the time to use your intuition. Check it to confirm your choice. Does the candidate feel right for the job? If you have nagging doubts despite a seemingly good fit, your intuition is telling you to slow down. Try to identify what's bothering you. Skills? Experience? Character? The candidate seems too perfect? Do another interview, check another reference, but don't hire until you feel good about a candidate.

If No Candidate Shines . . .

If none of your candidates stands out as a good prospect, don't hire. It's less painful in the long run to leave a position unfilled than to hire poorly.

Go back and look at the résumés you set aside earlier. Maybe there are a couple of possibilities you overlooked. (But don't relax your standards just to avoid starting the search over.)

If none seems suitable, go back to the search stage. Before you relaunch the search, however, take a few minutes to go over the job description and achievement factors. Are you asking for the impossible? Is the job fuzzy and in need of sharpening?

Make the Offer

When you're sure you have the right person, pounce. You've already set a salary range, so it won't be hard to come up with an appropriate starting salary based on skills and experience, and any other information you gleaned in the interview.

If you feel you may have to sell the job, or if you want to emphasize the ceremonial aspect of offering a job, call in the candidate so you can make the offer in person. Otherwise, do it by phone.

Explain the job again, and outline salary and benefits and any other perks that come with it. You've already talked about this with the candidate, so nothing should come as a surprise. Emphasize the job's growth possibilities and its opportunities to develop skills. In your zeal to sell, however, don't forget to talk about what you expect the person to contribute to the organization.

Caution: U.S. courts put a lot of emphasis on "implied contracts" in the employment arena. Don't promise anything you can't deliver, or anything you may have to change your mind about. For example, don't say, "This will lead to a managerial position in about two years," even if that's the case.

A candidate will often want time to think the offer over. Give a few days, but no more. You need to fill the position, and you don't want the candidate to go out searching for something better in the meantime.

Send Negotiators Packing

For most positions and most people, take it as a bad sign if someone wants to negotiate for more salary—either on the spot, or after a day or two of thinking it over. Career books counsel job seekers to go for the jugular once they know you want them. "You'll never have more power," they say. "Use it."

I think that's lousy advice. Is it worth it to a new jobholder to get an additional $1,000 or even $4,000 extra per year if it casts a cloud over what should be a pleasant honeymoon?

When I worked for others, I made it a point to take the salary offered. It starts the relationship off on a good foot. Besides, I figured I'd get paid what I was worth before long. And that was always the case.

The books are right, to some extent. It is hard to walk away from a candidate you worked hard to produce. Think twice, nonetheless, about haggling with an employee before he proves his worth to you. If you negotiate now, every dealing with the employee may be a negotiation.

Best Tip

Beware of those who want to haggle with you before they have proved their worth.

Say, "I'm sorry. That's what we're prepared to pay for your services right now."

The advice just given doesn't count when you're facing a truly superior candidate, one that will have an immediate, positive impact on the organization, and someone you know could step out the door and find another excellent job in short order. (And someone who knows it herself.)

If you can't come to terms with your number-one choice, and you don't have a close "second best," you may be forced back into the search stage. Grit your teeth and go to work.

Incidentally, one of the best co-workers I ever had, and someone who provided tremendous value to the company, was a second choice. Sometimes fate keeps you from making a mistake.

Start Off With Style

Organizations often miss a great opportunity to cement the enthusiasm and loyalty of new employees, and to make them productive early.

Seizing that opportunity is easy—just lavish attention on the employee for the first few days or weeks of the job.

To get the benefits, do the following:

1. Send a welcoming letter. Your new employee will be feeling a little uncertain. Send a letter immediately after offering the job and before the new person starts. In it, outline the job's particulars and express your pleasure with the decision.

2. Hold a first-morning orientation session. Make the new hire's first day special. Take her around first thing to meet other people in the work group. Give a tour of the building. Introduce her to a boss or other senior manager. Show her her office or desk, pointing out where to get water and supplies. Have her workmates convene mid-morning for coffee.

3. Have a first-day meeting. In it:

- Explain your personal values. "We all work hard around here, but we like to have fun. And I expect integrity in all things—from dealing with fellow employees to dealing with customers and vendors."
- Explain the company's vision, mission, and values if there are any. (But don't bother if these things are dusty and mostly unused.)
- Explain the department's or company's goals in precise terms. "Last year we had sales of $6.5 million, and we're aiming to sell $7.5 million this year. That's an important goal around here, so we track sales weekly."

- Explain your expectations for the new hire in precise terms. "I expect you to be able to sell about $10,000 worth of goods each week. I'll also expect you to open up at least ten new accounts this year."
- Explain how you like to work. "I'm pretty much hands-off as a manager. I set goals—and I expect you to meet them—but I step back and let you meet them your own way and in your own time. I generally don't step in unless I see a problem or unless you ask for help."
- Explain the benefits of success. "After six months, you'll be eligible for our bonus system. The employee manual explains how the bonus is figured. In good years, most of us double our salaries thanks to the system."

4. **Assign the new hire a "buddy" to spend a few days with.** This is most useful for lower-level positions like order-entry, making beds, or waiting tables. Nothing teaches as well as going through a couple of days with an experienced hand.

5. **Set them loose to work.** You've explained your values, given them goals, and offered help when they need it. Now let them loose to perform.

The Agile Manager's Checklist

✔ When you can't decide among qualified candidates, go back to the achievement factors. Who is strongest in the most important areas?

✔ Do one last check for illegal bias before offering a job.

✔ A final test: Does your intuition tell you that you're making the right choice?

✔ Negotiate salary upward only with extraordinary candidates.

✔ Make the new hire feel at home in your department from day one.

Index